WITHDRAWN

Cloudy Days

By Jennifer S. Burke

Children's Press
A Division of Grolier Publishing
New York / London / Hong Kong / Sydney
Danbury, Connecticut

Photo Credits: Cover and all photos by Thaddeus Harden
Contributing Editor: Mark Beyer
Book Design: Nelson Sa

Visit Children's Press on the Internet at:
http://publishing.grolier.com

Cataloging-in-Publication Data

Burke, Jennifer S.
    Cloudy days / by Jennifer S. Burke.
      p. cm. – (Weather report)
    Includes bibliographical references and index.
    Summary: Simple text and photographs present cloudy day activities.
    ISBN 0-516-23117-0 (lib. bdg.) – ISBN 0-516-23042-5 (pbk.)
    1. Clouds – Juvenile literature 2. Weather –
Juvenile literature [1. Clouds 2. Weather] I. Title
II. Series
    2000
551.57'6—dc21

Copyright © 2000 by Rosen Book Works, Inc.
All rights reserved. Published simultaneously in Canada.
Printed in the United States of America.
1 2 3 4 5 6 7 8 9 10 R 05 04 03 02 01 00

Contents

I can't see the sun today.

It is covered by **clouds**.

4

5

There are clouds everywhere.

It is not very light outside.

My mother and I were going to go to the **beach** today.

A cloudy day is not a good day for the beach.

9

My mother says, "There are other things to do on cloudy days."

She asks, "What else would you like to do?"

I ask my mother if we can go to the **playground**.

She says we can go to the playground.

She says I should wear a hat.

13

The clouds may go away.

The sun may come out.

My hat will **shade** my eyes.

14

15

It is cloudy, but I have fun at the playground.

I like to play on the swings.

17

My **shadow** is hard to see on cloudy days.

There is not enough sun to make my shadow clear.

Hey, look!

The clouds are breaking up.

The sun is showing through the clouds.

It is a nice day after all.

20

New Words

beach (**beech**) a place near water with sand or rocks

clouds (**clowdz**) puffy white or gray forms that float in the sky

playground (**play**-grownd) a place for kids to play on grass, or on swings and slides

shade (**shayd**) to make a spot that is not in sunlight

shadow (**shad**-oh) the shade made by something that is in front of the sun

To Find Out More

Books
Clouds
by Roy Wandelmaier and John Jones
Troll Communications

Hi, Clouds
by Carole Greene and Gene Sharp
Children's Press

The Cloud Book
by Tomie De Paola
Holiday House

Web Sites
Cloudy Skies
http://www.cloudyskies.net/clouds.html
Learn all about the different types of clouds on this site. There are many pictures of clouds you can look at.

Weather Gone Wild
http://tqjunior.advanced.org/5818
Find out all about the weather on this site. It tells about many different kinds of weather, including clouds.

Index

About the Author
Jennifer S. Burke is a teacher and a writer living in New York City. She holds a master's degree in reading education from Queens College, New York.

Reading Consultants
Kris Flynn, Coordinator, Small School District Literacy, The San Diego County Office of Education

Shelly Forys, Certified Reading Recovery Specialist, W.J. Zahnow Elementary School, Waterloo, IL

Peggy McNamara, Professor, Bank Street College of Education, Reading and Literacy Program